HOW TO DEAL WITH A MILITARY DIVORCE

A Handbook Of Rules And Regulations That Affect Your Case

Mitchell J. Howie, Esq.

Copyright © 2019 by Mitchell J. Howie, Esq.

All rights reserved. No part of this publication may be reproduced, distributed, or transmitted in any form or by any means, including photocopying, recording, or other electronic or mechanical methods, without the prior written permission of the publisher, except in the case of brief quotations embodied in critical reviews and certain other noncommercial uses permitted by copyright law. For permission requests, write to the publisher, addressed "Attention: Permissions Coordinator," at the address below.

Jacobs & Whitehall
73-03 Bell Blvd, #10
Oakland Gardens, NY 11364
www.jacobsandwhitehall.com

Ordering Information:

Quantity sales. Special discounts are available on quantity purchases by corporations, associations, and others. For details, contact the publisher at the address above.

Orders by U.S. trade bookstores and wholesalers. Please contact Jacobs & Whitehall: Tel: **(888)** 570-7338 or visit www.jacobsandwhitehall.com.

Printed in the United States of America

Published in 2019

ISBN: 978-1-946481-88-7

FOREWORD

I have wanted to write a book since I was a kid. Of course, I wanted to write a novel or some thriller that would actively engage and entertain readers. While my first debut as a published author is a far cry from a John Grisham courtroom drama I envisioned writing, I hope that this informative book helps those that are going through a dark time get information that they need when they need it! I also hope this book helps guide individuals to the best representation they can get in whatever state their divorce is occurring, so our military members and their families get the best possible individual results and family results as they transition from one sort of family life to another.

Dedication

This book is dedicated to all our military members (and their families) who serve this great country day in and day out. Only 1 percent of our population actually raise their hand to serve our great nation and I commend every one of our servicemembers for that service! And of course, I understand that the military member's family also serves in many respects. I hope that this book will help many military members and military families who are going through a difficult time in their lives. Military life has many hardships and unfortunately divorce is sometimes an unavoidable consequence of the constant military stressors (i.e. Deployments, Temporary Duties, other family separations, and constantly relocating the family). It is my sincere belief that his book will help those enduring these hardships.

ACKNOWLEDGEMENTS

Of course, I want to thank my wife (Melanie) for her constant commitment to our own military family (with nearly 5 years of active duty time as a family) and for continuing to make things work at home while I continue to serve in the Reserves (going on 10 years now!) Words cannot express how lucky I am to have you in my life and how lucky the kids are to have you as their mother. Thanks for all you do every day my most important military spouse! I also want to thank all of my active duty and reserve military bosses who have helped guide and mentor me during my military career. You all know who you are and how you have impacted me! Finally, I want to thank all of my past clients who have trusted me with handling your affairs. I am eternally grateful for all of you allowing me to get you to the "other side" and start life again. One military divorce client was part of the inspiration of this book as she really got a "raw deal" in a military divorce after 20 years of marriage. Fortunately, after 3 years of fighting, we were able to get what she should have received if she came to my office first!

DISCLAIMER

This publication is intended to be used for educational purposes only. No legal advice is being given, and no attorney-client relationship is intended to be created by reading this material. The author assumes no liability for any errors or omissions or for how this book or its contents are used or interpreted or for any consequences resulting directly or indirectly from the use of this book. For legal or any other advice, please consult an experienced attorney or the appropriate expert who is aware of the specific facts of your case and is knowledgeable of the law in your jurisdiction.

Law Office of Mitchell J. Howie
107 North Side Square
Huntsville, Alabama 35801
www.mitchellhowie.com
(256) 533-8074

TESTIMONIALS

"Mitchell J. Howie is simply the best family lawyer in Huntsville, Alabama! I was searching for the best divorce lawyer in Huntsville and after reading his great reviews I decided to make an appointment. And he met all my expectations and even more! With his help I was able to ensure I was getting prompt and accurate advice on the multiple issues I was facing. With Mitchell J. Howie on my side, I got everything I wanted from the divorce and child custody case! If you need the best family attorney in Huntsville, you should call Mitchell J. Howie. He was kind and caring about my situation and always promptly returned my e-mails and calls. I can't thank him enough!"

— *C.*

****

"Highly recommended divorce attorney! I was being sued for an incredibly large (for me) amount of money 13 years after my divorce! Mr. Howie helped me get the situation resolved. He was diligent in my defense and didn't wait to get things done! I'm glad to have had him on my side."

— ***Gil C.***

****

"Unfortunately, I'm experiencing a late in life divorce...with a young child and a military disability pension. I'm not from the area, and had no knowledge of the attorneys that practice in this area. This led me to several attorney's...purely out of random selection. The first firm, I found out...had no experience in military disability pensions. The second firm I tried, had a person with the proper credentials and experience for my unique situation...but, she had more cases than she could manage, at the time. BUT, she pointed me to Mitchell Howie. Mitchell has been a blessing to me. He's a former Air Force JAG and still serves as a Reservist. He's extremely knowledgeable in Military Law and Family Law...I understand he is also an expert in some other areas of the law. He's passionate in representing his clients...and a "straight shooter". He's bright, energetic and dedicated. He actually called me back for my first phone consultation, while his office was closed over the New Year's Holiday. I highly recommend Mitchell Howie as your attorney."

—*Anthony Henderson*

****

"Mitchell and his staff are very quick to answer your questions and concerns in a timely manner. I felt like he and his firm really cared about my situation and handled my case as if I was their top priority. Would definitely recommend him!!"

— *David*

****

"I strongly endorse this lawyer! I have had the pleasure of teaching trial advocacy with Mitchell Howie all over the globe as part of our duty in the military. We have taught classes in Korea and Germany together and I am always impressed by his knowledge on the law and the tips he provides students. Even though I have been practicing law for over 11 years, I often found myself jotting down many of the tips he gives students! He is a gifted trial advocate instructor and will absolutely go the extra mile for his clients! I highly recommend Mitch! You should definitely pick the law offices of Mitchell john Howie to help you with your legal issues!"

*— **Andre***

****

"Mr. Howie is the best military divorce lawyer in Huntsville! He provided me the best representation I could have asked for. His attention to detail and knowledge of military law came to be priceless in my case. I am truly thankful for his services during this life-changing event. I will continue to seek his guidance if needed in the future."

*— **Ruby***

****

TABLE OF CONTENTS

i.	**Foreword**	3
ii.	**Dedication**	4
iii.	**Acknowledgements**	5
iv.	**Disclaimer**	6
v.	**Testimonials**	7
vi.	**About The Author**	13
1.	**Difference Between A Military Divorce & A Civilian Divorce**	15
2.	**What Is The Process To File For A Military Divorce?**	19
3.	**Residency Requirement To File For Divorce In Alabama**	22
4.	**Factors That Might Impact A Military Divorce**	28

5.	**What If I Am Overseas And Cannot Attend Hearings?**	**32**
6.	**How Does Military Service Affect Child Custody?**	**34**
7.	**Parenting Plan — What Are The Options?**	**38**
8.	**Different Levels Of Child Support Guidelines**	**40**
9.	**Can Custody Or Child Support Orders Be Modified?**	**44**
10.	**Is Alimony Or Spousal Support Granted Automatically?**	**46**
11.	**Is My Spouse Entitled To My Military Benefits And Retirement Pay?**	**48**
12.	**Dividing Assets And Debts In A Military Divorce**	**51**
13.	**Will I Be Able To Keep My Military ID After A Divorce?**	**53**

14.	**Can A Final Military Divorce Decree Be Modified?**	**55**
15.	**Why Hire An Experienced Military Divorce Lawyer?**	**57**
vii.	**What Is The Next Step?**	**60**
viii.	**Index**	**61**
ix.	**Notes**	**63**

ABOUT THE AUTHOR

I've been a practicing lawyer since 2004. I originally opened my practice in Texas, but I still really wanted to serve in the military. I almost went to the Naval Academy directly out of high school and the urge to serve in the military only grew as I got older. I ended up going into the JAG Corps after I had already opened my own practice. I was on active duty for almost five years in the Air Force. Since that time, I've been serving in the reserves and I currently teach trial advocacy to younger JAGs at various military installations around the globe.

As far as my experience in handling military divorces, I received my first experience when I was serving on active duty, as a legal assistant attorney. I dealt with hundreds of clients who needed to know the basics of military divorce and how it could affect their careers and their lives.

Once I left active duty and I re-opened my own firm, I knew I wanted to help people who had served in the military with military divorces. Since I've been in private practice, I've helped a lot of military members and military families from beginning to end with their divorce cases. I am passionate about this work and continuing to serve those who serve our nation along with their families!

CHAPTER 1

DIFFERENCE BETWEEN A MILITARY DIVORCE & A CIVILIAN DIVORCE

The biggest difference between a military divorce and a civilian divorce is obviously that either one spouse, or both of the spouses are currently serving (or at some point did serve) in the military. Of course, divorces are ultimately controlled by state law and whichever state you're filing in is going to dictate the divorce law that applies. However, with military members, you can have specific jurisdictional issues and residency requirements when determining where to file and when to file. You can have military justice issues.

When you have allegations of domestic violence, child abuse, or adultery, which is a crime under UCMJ, you certainly want your divorce lawyer to be familiar with the military justice system.

In military divorces, there are a lot of additional considerations that most civilian family law practitioners are not as well versed in as those who have served in the military, or those that have chosen to devote a large part of their practice to military divorce. For instance, there are specific regulations on how to divide a thrift savings plan. There's the specific procedures on how and when to ensure the equitable division of a military retirement, which oftentimes, is the largest asset in someone's marital estate. The rules and regulations that go along with that are critical to effectively handling a military divorce.

Additionally, military divorces are different because deployments and temporary duty assignments (TDYs) have the potential to affect child custody considerations. Alabama actually has a specific statute that's meant to protect military members from having their service to this country harm their ability to raise their kids and be considered as a primary placement or sole physical custodian. Clearly a military member involved in a divorce with these issues is going to need a good military divorce lawyer to deal with the specific issues of deployments and temporary duties taking a military member away from their family. Many of these issues could be very important considerations in a divorce or child custody case. If you haven't lived through that, you may not understand the difference between a TDY, and a permanent change of station, and you certainly do not really comprehend how hard deployments can be on a family. These intricate issues are the things that someone going through a military divorce needs their lawyer to understand completely.

Do We Need A Reason To File For Military Divorce?

A divorce is only a military divorce because one, or both of the spouses, happens to be a military member. It's still just a divorce, as far as your individual state is concerned. The reasons that you would need to file for divorce from a military member are the same as the reasons for any other divorce. Maybe you don't get along anymore. Perhaps someone has cheated or become abusive. All of those issues that can cause the breakdown of a marriage are the same in a military marriage as they are in a civilian one. The difference is you want a military divorce lawyer, who knows about all of the intricacies of military life and the interplay between federal statutes, state statutes, military service, and the potential impact upon the divorce proceedings.

Is There A Required Waiting Period In a Military Divorce?

Whether or not there is a waiting or separation period required in a divorce depends on which state the divorce is filed. For example, North Carolina (where I served as an assistant judge advocate at Pope Air Force Base) requires a separation period; Alabama does not. Determining if there is a waiting period in a specific state is one of the criteria you will want your military divorce lawyer to consider before choosing a state to file the divorce (if you are in a situation where a choice of an individual state is possible due to the parties' military service).

Chapter 2

What Is The Process To File For A Military Divorce?

To file for a military divorce (or a civilian divorce), in Alabama, you file your complaint and you allege the grounds, be it an irretrievable breakdown, which is "no fault" grounds, or you allege fault, such as adultery or cruelty. There's a statute that lists all the possible grounds for divorce in Alabama. After you have your spouse served, they have 30 days to respond. From that point, you go through the discovery period of depositions, interrogatories, requests for productions, and requests for admissions.

Where I practice, which is primarily in Huntsville, Alabama, if it's going to be a fully litigated trial, you're looking at a trial date six months away, at the earliest. Usually, it will be closer to a year, or a year and a half before you are reached on a trial docket. When you get to a trial docket and you have your day (or days) before the judge, the judge will issue an order and then will give you a final divorce decree. At that point, you will finally be legally divorced from your spouse.

That is the contested route. There is also the much quicker process of an uncontested divorce. An uncontested divorce is right for you if you and your spouse are in agreement on your military divorce and you have all of the issues worked out, such as division of military retirement, division of the TSP, alimony, child custody, child support and an equitable division of the assets and debts. If that agreement is provided to me, I will file it and the judge is supposed to get you a final decree of divorce within 30 days. Uncontested divorces are much cheaper, much quicker, and much simpler. I often tell clients that the only certain winners in full blown litigated divorce trials are the lawyers. However, sometimes an uncontested divorce is impossible due to hurt feelings and raw emotions as the process begins but as time passes even a contested divorce can settle as an uncontested divorce at some point in the process once "cooler heads prevail."

CHAPTER 3

RESIDENCY REQUIREMENT TO FILE FOR DIVORCE IN ALABAMA

The residency requirement in Alabama, to file for divorce is six months. The intricate issue that comes up in a military divorce is that you could be stationed somewhere else from your home of record, or you could have property in another state, or due to military service you have made another state your home state and become a resident of that state. Basically, you can file in the state where the servicemember is currently stationed, or if you meet the six-month residency requirement in Alabama, you can file in the state where the servicemember claims legal residency, or sometimes the spouse can file where the non-military spouse resides while the servicemember is deployed or TDY to another location. Sometimes the servicemember can object using the Servicemember's Civil Relief Act protections, however, other times the servicemember wants the divorce to be done as quickly as possible and therefore does not raise any objection.

As an example, let's say that a 20-year-old girl meets a JAG officer who's training in Montgomery. They are both from Huntsville, but they meet in Montgomery. She follows him to North Carolina, to Rhode Island, and to Texas. Eventually, after they have children, he becomes abusive. She comes back home to Huntsville and has been living there for six months with the children, while he's still off serving. She would likely want to file in Alabama to get jurisdiction where she's going to have her support network. There are a lot of strategic and tactical decisions that need to be made when deciding where to file when you have a military member who's serving all over the country.

What If My Spouse And I Are Living In Different States At The Time We Want To File For Divorce? Where Do I File?

In a situation where the spouses live in different states, I file wherever it benefits my client. There are jurisdictional issues created by the inherent transitional nature of the military life and you want your military divorce lawyer to thoroughly understand and be capable of properly analyzing those issues.

As another example on deciding where to file, Alabama used to have a 10-year requirement before the Court could even divide military retirement. That meant that the marriage had to be at least 10 years long before retirement assets could be divided. In that case, if you're in the military and your largest asset is your military retirement, and you've been married for nine years, you would want to file in Alabama. Because in Alabama during the divorce your military retirement pension would be off the table! Unfortunately for some that law was changed recently but you've got to look at factors like that.

Now, in Alabama, we have a law that says retirement assets are divisible just like anything else and there's no time prohibition for dividing those assets. However, if you're in Alabama (or whatever State you are considering and capable of filing in), you still want to consider whether filing in that particular state is going to be cheaper than filing in other potential state(s) and make the best decision based on your individual circumstances.

If My Spouse Is Serving Overseas, Do I Need To Wait To File For A Divorce?

You don't have to wait to file for divorce, if your spouse is serving overseas. A problem that may be encountered is the Servicemembers Civil Relief Act (SCRA). When someone is serving overseas, if I'm representing the spouse and they want to file for divorce, I tell them we can absolutely still file **after** we determine strategically that is the best course of action. (Oftentimes it makes sense to wait until the servicemember returns from overseas.)

On the other hand, when I am representing a servicemember who is serving overseas who has been served with divorce papers, I tell them that they need to get a SCRA letter, which is a stay letter from the commander.

Then, I can convey that letter to the court, in order for them to get the protections afforded them by federal law to stay the proceedings against them. It really does not make any sense for a servicemember to have to deal with divorce while they are overseas serving our country. A skilled military divorce lawyer should do everything in their power to ensure that Soldier, Sailor, Marine and/or Airman's divorce is continued so the military member can focus on what is important until they return back home safely. That is certainly my practice!

The intent of SCRA is that we don't want military members overseas fighting a war and also having to worry about civil matters at home. A spouse can file for divorce but, most likely, what's going to happen is a SCRA stay will be issued and then the court will not address the divorce until the military member is back in the country. From a strategic standpoint, if my client is hit with a divorce while they're serving overseas, I certainly try to portray the other side as callous and unpatriotic by having the audacity to serve my client, who is serving our country overseas, with a divorce, therefore taking them away from the mission at hand.

Is Where You File A Military Divorce Important?

When deciding where to file for divorce, you've got to look at the state law and see if there's any benefit to filing in one state versus another. It's an important consideration that you want an attorney to be able to examine on the front end. For example, North Carolina, has a required separation period of a year. When people are ready to get divorced, they don't want to wait a whole year. In Alabama, there's no legal separation period. You can file for divorce, even when you are still living together so long as you can represent you are separated and intend to terminate the marriage. Those are the kinds of considerations you want to have your attorney look at before you file for divorce.

CHAPTER 4

FACTORS THAT MIGHT IMPACT A MILITARY DIVORCE

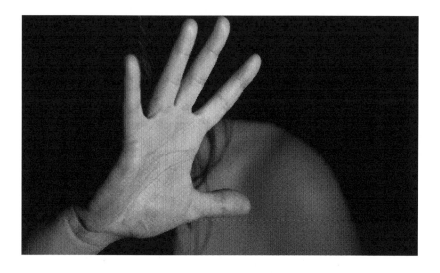

Adultery is a crime under the UCMJ. Oftentimes, it makes a lot of sense for a spouse to admit to adultery because there may be overwhelming evidence to prove the adultery. You certainly don't want a client to lie and then go before a judge and make the judge wonder what else the client is lying about. If that happens you could end up getting hammered in the divorce decree. You have a right to invoke your constitutional rights: your right to remain silent and your Fifth Amendment Rights to not answer any questions in discovery about adultery or domestic violence.

You want your attorney to be aware of the major impacts that an allegation of adultery could have on your career. Even if the command doesn't want to prosecute you in the military justice system, they could hit you with a letter of reprimand, which could lead to an administrative discharge. Then, your military career is over simply because you didn't invoke your right to not incriminate yourself.

Issues of domestic violence are also important in the military because there's the Lautenberg Amendment, which dictates that anyone who is convicted of a domestic violence charge, even if it is a misdemeanor, becomes unable to legally carry a firearm. At that point obviously the military member's career in the military is over. If you are prevented by federal law from carrying a firearm, you're not going to be of much use to the military. In a military divorce, you want your attorney to know what the UCMJ is and what punitive articles are in the UCMJ that may not be in the civilian criminal justice system. You want your attorney to know what an Article 15 is and what the process is for an

Article 15 and what are the effects on a military member's career from an Article 15. You need your military attorney to know what a "LOR" and "LOC" stands for, and what the consequences of a letter of reprimand are versus the consequences of a letter of counseling. You need an attorney who knows what a PIF is and the consequences upon one's career from having derogatory data in their personal information file.

If I'm representing a spouse, it's a major advantage to know which levers need to be pulled in order to put pressure on the military member. If I'm representing the military member, I know the pitfalls and the landmines that we're trying to avoid, as we go through the military divorce process.

Does Filing First For A Divorce Matter?

A lot of people think that being the plaintiff in a family law situation gives you an advantage because it means you're going to be able to testify first before the Judge. Perhaps what comes out first sticks in the judge's mind the best, but I don't know if I agree with that idea. It is just one consideration to take into account.

In many cases, I have seen a male spouse file for divorce and then that party was retaliated against by his spouse. In other case, I have seen the female spouse file first and then proceed to attempt to involve the military member's command in every single action moving forward.

It is probably always a good practice as a military member to go to your command and warn them that your spouse has filed for divorce against you and may be attempting to make you look bad in the near future. A lot of military members look at divorce as just part of the job and an unfortunate part of military life. And you cannot be a commander in the military for longer than "one minute" and not have to deal with a contentious divorce or some aspect of a military member's divorce proceedings.

CHAPTER 5

WHAT IF I AM OVERSEAS AND CANNOT ATTEND HEARINGS?

If you are serving overseas and cannot attend your divorce hearing, you would have your commander write a SCRA letter, indicating that you're unable to participate in the divorce proceedings. Then, you're going to want your attorney to get the commander's letter in front of the judge, or to file a special appearance requesting the stay, but notifying the court that you're going to contest jurisdiction. This comes up a lot when you have someone who's going overseas and then the spouse wants to gain a tactical advantage while that military member is serving. In that situation, you want and need a stay of the proceedings under the Servicemembers Civil Relief Act.

For example, let's say a military couple is living in Texas. They have children there. The father is serving in Iraq for six months. The mother dis-enrolls the kids from school because she has a boyfriend in Alabama. She moves to Alabama, which is where her family is from. She files for divorce in Alabama (after maintaining residency for six months) and then proceeds to have her spouse served with a divorce in Alabama and he's never even lived in Alabama. There's no reason at all for Alabama to have jurisdiction. He would want to hire an Alabama attorney to request a stay of the proceedings and to file a motion to dismiss the action filed in Alabama. He would then probably want to try to get an attorney to file a divorce in Texas (which is where the children had lived for the last two or three years and where the marital home was when he left to go overseas).

CHAPTER 6

HOW DOES MILITARY SERVICE AFFECT CHILD CUSTODY?

Every military member with children is required to have a family care plan. This is a detailed plan as to what's going to happen when and if you are deployed or go TDY. You have to designate responsible people, typically your spouse, to take care of the children. The factors that the court considers for child custody are what is in the "best interests of the child." Any factor that can determine what's in the best interest of the child is something that can be looked at by a court when making a custody determination.

All aspects of home life can be investigated: the location, the personal relationship between the parents, and the relationship between the parents and the child, who helps the kids with homework, who cooks for the kids, who disciplines the kids, all of these things will be examined. Courts consider the parental interest of the parent in the children. If one parent has been involved throughout the child's life, while the other parent has been taking voluntary deployments, the court is going to look to the parent who's been there as the primary caretaker. They're more likely to award sole physical custody to that person because they've shown an interest in their child. Other factors are mental health and stability.

Another factor considered by Courts is, oftentimes, expert opinions. If there are allegations of abuse, experts can be relied upon to testify to the court. Additionally, one unique statutory protection for military members in Alabama affecting custody cases is Alabama Code Section 30-3-9 which says that military deployment may not be the sole factor in a child custody determination. The question becomes how military service can impact the court in analyzing the factors in a custody case. You want your attorney to be aware of that and how that will affect and impact the trial court's "best interest analysis" of all the factors considered.

Can A Child Have Any Say In The Parent He Or She Wants To Live With?

Most judges agree (and the law holds) that the preference of a child younger than 12 years of age isn't going to be listened to in a custody case. Obviously, a judge can decide to listen to a child and if a child is talking about abuse, their input is going to be considered. As far as a child just wanting to go with Mom or Dad, the judge may give that some consideration, but it will typically not be a deciding factor. Even with older children, the weight of the child's opinion is limited to the maturity of the child and do we really believe judges are going to let teenagers choose what they want to do?

Could I Obtain Custody Of My Children Even Though I Am Assigned To A Deployable Unit?

As long as you can show that you have a plan in place for the care of your child, you can obtain custody. Alabama has a code section ensuring that the military deployment of a military member is not the only factor to be considered in a child custody determination that provides some protection on this issue. However, the reality exists where one spouse is not in the military and is a suitable and fit parent and one spouse is in the military and is deployed. In that situation, the other parent will obviously be determined as the fit and proper parent to take care of the children while the spouse is deployed.

Chapter 7
Parenting Plan — What Are the Options?

A parenting plan, whether part of a military or a civilian divorce, is obviously going to be limited by whether Dad or Mom is traveling frequently for their employment. If Dad is the primary caregiver and the homemaker, a court is going to award sole physical custody to him because he's the one at home to raise the child. I've had many cases where the military member is deployed and up until that point, the deployed military member had been the primary sole physical custodian of the child. However, the spouse knew that once the member was deployed for a year, it was a good strategic time to file for divorce to try to get sole physical custody of the children. Obviously the timing of the filing, and the military member's absence, is a potent tool that can sometimes be used to the detriment of the spouse serving in the military.

On the other hand, if you can show that you're not deploying for the next three or four years and your kids are teenagers, you're going to have an opportunity to have the children just as much as your spouse. The options for a parenting plan are the same in a military divorce as they are for people who are limited by their civilian employment. I've seen plans where one member is serving and they're going to be deployed a lot, so an agreement is made that once the military member is back, they're going to have an extensive amount of time with the child.

Chapter 8
Different Levels Of Child Support Guidelines

All of the services have different regulations, requiring different levels of support, and it doesn't have to be children. It can be dependents, including spouses. The Air Force regulation, when I was on active duty, required "reasonable support" to dependents. Typically, first sergeants, JAGs, and commanders determined that reasonable support was the difference between BAH (basic allowance for housing) with dependents and BAH without dependents. However, recently the Air Force has amended that regulation.

Now, there's a calculation that is very much in line with what the Army has always done, which requires much more overall support to dependents. One strategic thing that you want your military divorce lawyer to be tracking is what those specific regulations are when it comes to the payment and receipt of support. Oftentimes, in a brief marriage that does not have any children, it is to the spouse's benefit to drag out the divorce because they're going to get more support money under military regulations than they will under state law, once the divorce is final.

Will My Children Be Entitled To Military Benefits After A Divorce?

As long as your children are dependents and they are in the Defense Enrollment Eligibility Reporting System (DEERS), they should still get military benefits. That's another strategic issue that you will want your lawyer to handle. Sometimes, it makes sense to keep kids in DEERS for the military member because you want the children to have the benefits provided by Tri-Care. Even after the divorce, your children can still get military benefits.

What Is A Leave And Earnings Statement?

When you're dealing with child support in a military family, you need someone who can read a leave and earnings statement (LES). If you don't have experience reading leave and earnings statements, they can be confusing. You want an attorney who knows how to request one, knows what they're looking at, and knows how to get documents from the Defense Financial Accounting Service (DFAS). You want someone who can determine exactly how much a military member is making because sometimes tax returns don't tell the whole story. If an attorney doesn't know that a promotion to O-6 comes with a significant pay increase, they're not going to be able to prove that substantial increase in income and get their client the corresponding increase in child support.

What Happens If My Military Ex-Spouse Refuses To Pay Child Support After Divorce?

If I'm representing a spouse and the military member has refused to pay child support, I know I can pretty much determine exactly how much he is supposed to be paying per military regulations prior to the divorce. Of course the divorce decree would indicate how much he should be paying after the divorce. If necessary I know how and when to go to the military member's first sergeant, or to the commander, and let them know that this person is not paying what they need to pay. If your attorney doesn't have that knowledge, you're going to have to go through the normal process of having to file something in family law court requesting an emergency hearing. However, there are regulations that require servicemembers to reasonably support their spouse and dependents, even before the divorce is final. You will certainly want your military divorce lawyer to understand those regulations to get you the best possible results.

CHAPTER 9
CAN CUSTODY OR CHILD SUPPORT ORDERS BE MODIFIED?

Family law orders related to custody or child support are always modifiable. All you need to allege is a "material change in circumstances" in Alabama, and you can go back to court. Let's take another example, Nancy is in the army and she deploys for a year and a half. She keeps getting extended on her deployments. She had been the primary caretaker prior to the deployment but the husband gets an agreement from her for him to be the sole physical custodian, meaning the children will live with him during the week. Visitation will be given to Nancy when she's back from deployment. Nancy, unfortunately, gets hit with an IED and loses her leg. She comes back on 100% disability but she's now able to be the primary caretaker again. At that point, there has been a material change in circumstances. Since Nancy is no longer serving in the military you would hope that her husband would agree to allow her to become the sole physical custodian or have a true joint legal custody arrangement. If he does not agree, Nancy could file for a modification of the child custody arrangement and she would plead the facts as outlined above. A judge would, hopefully, see it her way and give her more time with the kids. Of course, the controlling factor is always going to be the best interest of the children.

Another consideration you want your divorce lawyer tracking is how and when the "McClendon Standard" comes into effect after someone has been provided sole physical custody. If someone is given sole physical custody, the McClendon Standard is typically invoked and then a party will have a higher burden to prove that a change in custody will outweigh the inherent disruption of the children's stability and routine.

Chapter 10

Is Alimony Or Spousal Support Granted Automatically?

Alimony or spousal support is not automatically granted in any divorce. In Alabama, a law has been passed that only allows alimony up to the length of the marriage. Accordingly, if you've been married for 10 years, the maximum amount of alimony that someone could pay is 10 years. Once a marriage has lasted for 20 years, the judge can consider ordering permanent alimony. The basic factors to be considered for an alimony award are the incomes of each party, the length of the marriage, the health of the parties, the ability of each party to earn, and the ability to pay and fault in the marriage.

Your attorney can give you a good read as to whether or not alimony will be considered in your case. The length of the marriage is a big factor in determining whether alimony will be ordered. However, you certainly want your military divorce lawyer to understand that while the divorce is pending, dependents are still entitled to support under military regulations.

Specifics Of Alimony Or Spousal Support If One Or Both Spouses Are In The Military

In any type of divorce, the court is going to look at what someone can pay before ordering them to pay an alimony award. The spouse has to be able to prove the "ability to pay" factor. With the military, it's easy to do. You get the LES and you determine exactly how much money that person has made. On the other hand, if one spouse is in the military and the other spouse owns a business, then you want to have an attorney who can track down that money earned through their individual business. You can typically do that through tax returns and profit loss statements and other accounting documents.

CHAPTER 11

IS MY SPOUSE ENTITLED TO MY MILITARY BENEFITS AND RETIREMENT PAY?

Military retirement pay can be divided just like any other asset in Alabama now. There's no time limit. I've had military members think that their spouse can't get their retirement because they were not married for 10 years. That's not actually the law and if you are a spouse trying to get those military benefits, you certainly want an attorney who understands what those military benefits are and how to calculate the present value of the military retirement asset.

When it comes to base access, ID privileges, and access to military healthcare and TRICARE, the big rule that you need to know is the 20/20/20 rule. That's 20 years of marriage, 20 years of military service, and 20 years of overlap between the marriage and the military service. Only then is a dependent entitled to a Military ID card with all the requisite benefits that come along with that.

You don't want to file for divorce if you've been married for 19 years and six months and you're fed up with your spouse. If you came into my office in that scenario, I would say you need to wait it out and not even mention divorce again until it's been 20 years. Healthcare and health expenses are the largest expense that you have in your older years and having that paid for by the government is invaluable.

With respect to spouses, you can get COBRA after a divorce. That's the Consolidated Omnibus Budget Reconciliation Act. With COBRA, you would have that as an access point for the spouse and for the children. The children can also stay on TRICARE as long as they're dependents in DEERS. Basically, they can stay on the parents' TRICARE until they're 26 years old.

What Should I Know About Marital Shares in Military Pension Division?

The National Defense Authorization Act of 2017 has come to be known as the "frozen benefits rule" for military retirement division. Military retirement has historically been divided based on state laws. The Uniformed Former Spouses Protection Act allows the states to divide a military retirement as if it was any other asset. That was the law until 2017, when Congress decided to rewrite every state's law and make military retirement different from everything else. The current required method of military pension division now involves a hypothetical amount of retired pay which is calculated as if the military member retired on the date of the divorce decree being issued. In the new calculation the numerator is the number of years that you've been married, and the denominator is the amount of years of military service. If you're representing the military member, you want the denominator to be as big as possible. You want this to shrink to the other side's share of the total military retirement and the "frozen benefits rule" has absolutely helped with that.

CHAPTER 12

DIVIDING ASSETS AND DEBTS IN A MILITARY DIVORCE

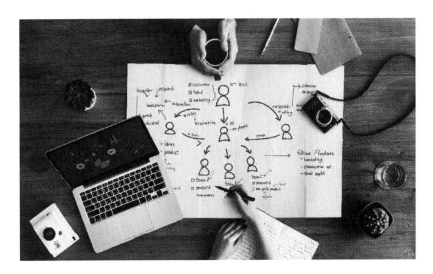

Debts are divided, in Alabama, based on equitable division. It is not a community property state. Community property is basically split 50/50. Alabama is an equitable division state, so the judges start at 50% and then, based on fault and the facts of the individual case, can give up to 100% to one spouse. The date of filing is important because it should lock in the time for division of debts and assets but that is state-law specific and depends on the circumstances of the case.

How Are Issues Pertaining To Division Of Assets And Debts Resolved In A Military Divorce?

In your pleadings, you can specify that there was separate property, such as an inheritance. If that separate property is not co-mingled, then your position with the judge is that it is not subject to equitable division. Separate property is an issue that you deal with in military divorces and in civilian divorces. If separate property has been co-mingled, meaning it has been used regularly for the benefit of the married couple. Then, it's subject to equitable division.

CHAPTER 13

WILL I BE ABLE TO KEEP MY MILITARY ID AFTER A DIVORCE?

Unless you meet the 20/20/20 rule as a spouse, you're not going to continue to have a military ID. Those are only for dependents, so the children will keep theirs, as long as they're in DEERS. One issue is when you have a spouse who has sole physical custody of the kids and they have to get on base to get their children's IDs updated, but they can't get on base because they don't have access. You need someone who's dealt with this issue before and who can tell you how to get a visitor's pass and can get your child's updated ID card.

Can I Continue To Receive Benefits Such As Housing Allowances After A Divorce?

The Basic Allowance for Housing (BAH) is dependent upon what rank you are, where you live, and other factors. As a dependent, you're not automatically entitled to it even when you're still married. Once you're divorced, in Alabama, you're subject to Rule 32 child support. There's a calculation and you just plug in how much money the spouse makes, how much money the military member makes, work related childcare expenses, and health care expenses and the formula will provide an amount due monthly for child support. Accordingly, you will know how much child support that person is supposed to pay.

You need your lawyer to run the Rule 32 calculation, if you're in Alabama, and also calculate the service specific requirement then choose which one benefits you during the pendency of the divorce. Obviously, you want your lawyer if you're the military member to help you pay less. If you are a spouse, you typically want the spouse to pay more.

CHAPTER 14

CAN A FINAL MILITARY DIVORCE DECREE BE MODIFIED?

In Alabama, you simply need to have a material change in circumstances to modify certain aspects of a divorce decree (issues that are modifiable typically include child custody issues, child support and spousal support issues but property divisions are non-modifiable in Alabama). If someone is no longer employed or they're no longer employed by the military, or they're making more or less money, those are considered a material change in circumstances. If someone goes to jail or becomes a drug addict, these factors can be used to plead a material change in circumstances to modify a previous decree. With the military, people move all the time. If you move closer to one another, you may want to get more physical custody time with your kids. You may need to try to insert a plan in the original order (if the Court will allow) for those certain changes you know are coming, so you're not having to go back to court all the time.

CHAPTER 15

WHY HIRE AN EXPERIENCED MILITARY DIVORCE LAWYER?

Military divorces involve a whole host of issues that are not encountered in a typical civilian divorce. For instance, Military retirement division, in particular, is extremely intricate and detailed. There are rules and regulations with respect to that pension division, including the 2017 NDAA. You need an attorney who knows what the survivor benefit plan is. You have to word the order appropriately or you could lose out on literally millions of dollars in benefits. Even some judges and experienced lawyers aren't aware of the exact language that needs to be used. You definitely need someone who is familiar with the survivor benefit plan to help you in a military divorce, if that's an issue.

You need someone who understands the military life: TDYs, temporary duty, permanent change of stations, PCS, and deployments. They need to understand the military justice system and administrative discharge processes. Of course, VA Disability and VA Awards are a big part of any military divorce and you need an attorney who understands all of these issues. If you, as a spouse, don't have a lawyer who understands that, the military member could pull one over on you, as far as division of military retirement goes. There is language that has to be inserted to either protect a spouse from getting a decrease in the military retirement or protect the military member from having to pay that entire military retirement award.

Your attorney needs to know what a "deemed election" is for a survivor benefit plan and what Servicemembers Government Life Insurance (SGLI) is. He or she should know that it's not divisible. You certainly want someone who is well versed in all of the jurisdictional and residency issues that you may have, so you're filing at the most opportune time and in the most opportune place, which benefits you and serves your goals for the divorce. I have heard many clients say that an experienced military divorce attorney can likely handle a typical civilian divorce, however, a civilian divorce attorney may not be able to handle all the intricate issues involved in a military divorce.

WHAT IS THE NEXT STEP?

If you would like to speak to a skilled military divorce lawyer you can reach our office by e-mailing us at info@mitchellhowie.com or calling us at 256-533-8074. A consultation fee will apply for nearly all cases.

INDEX

A

adultery · 28
alimony · 46

C

child support · 44
civilian divorce · 15
civilian employment · 39

D

divorce hearing · 32
domestic violence · 29

E

equitable division · 52

F

Fifth Amendment Rights · 28
final divorce decree · 20
first sergeant · 43
fully litigated trial · 20

I

inheritance · 52

J

jurisdictional issues · 24

L

leave and earnings statement · 42

M

marital estate · 16

military benefits · 48

military divorce · 15

Military ID · 49

military justice system · 58

misdemeanor · 29

P

parenting plan · 38

permanent alimony · 46

primary caretaker · 44

R

residency requirement · 22

retirement assets · 25

Rule 32 child support · 54

T

testify · 30

NOTES